24" Blue & Gold Flat Spiral Necklace

120 round 5mm matte clear blue acrylic beads
242 round 6mm textured gold beads
6⅔ yards of monofilament nylon
4 gold calotte crimps
1 gold 2-row box clasp
basic supplies (see inside the front cover)

1 Cut the nylon into two 10-foot lengths. Lay one on a flat surface and tape it down 4" from the right end. Follow the diagram to string beads until there are 72 beads in the first row. Tape the second length under the first. String the remaining beads until all have been used.

2 String a calotte onto one nylon end and slide it close to the last bead. Knot several times, until the knot is large enough not to pull through the hole. Seal the knot with nail polish; let dry. Cut off excess nylon close to the knot and use pliers to close the calotte. Repeat for the remaining three nylon ends.

3 On one end of the necklace, hook one calotte through each eye of a clasp section. Repeat on the other end of the necklace with the other clasp section.

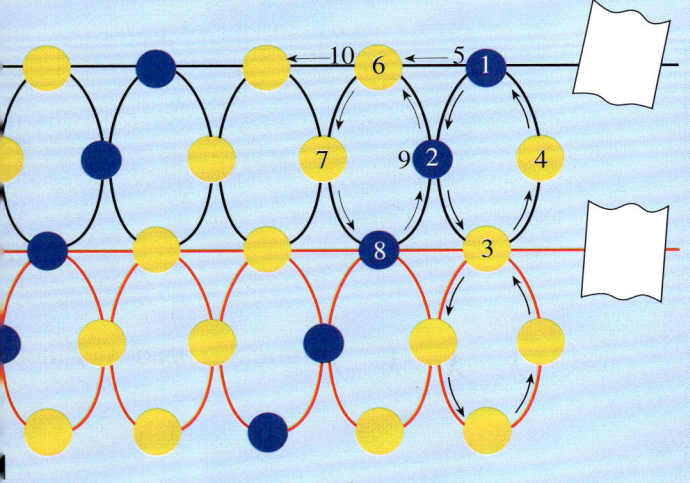

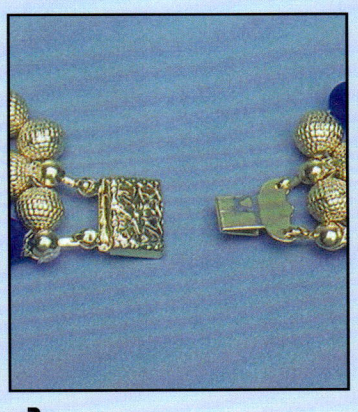

Blue & Silver Necklace

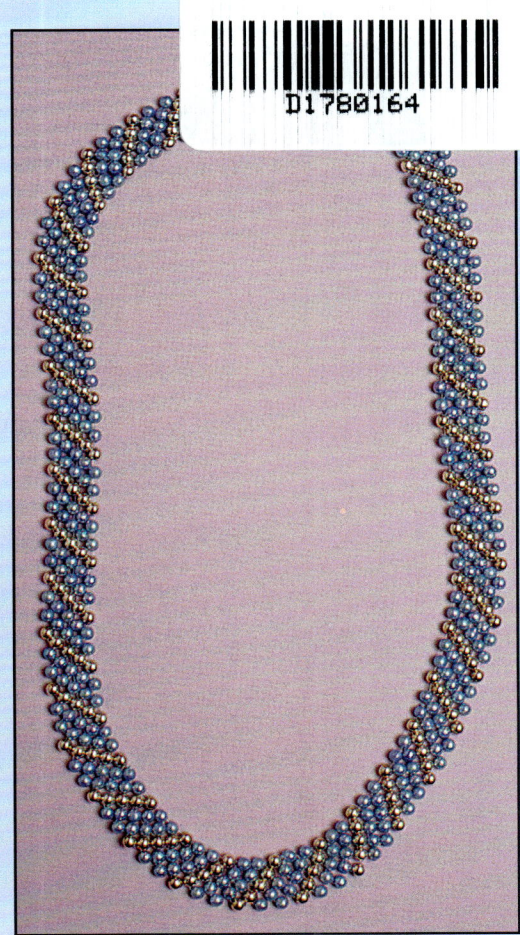

This 27" flat spiral necklace is woven from the same pattern as the one above, but uses 4mm round beads. You will need 179 silver beads and 360 iridescent light blue beads.

2 Single-Weave Adjustable Choker, Bracelet & Earrings

basic supplies
 (see inside the front cover)

16" choker:
4 round 4mm gold beads
81 round 6mm white pearls
41 round 6mm gold beads
2⅔ yards of monofilament nylon
10 gold 5mm jump rings
2 gold calotte crimps
1 gold head pin
1 gold clasp hook

7½" bracelet:
4 round 4mm gold beads
36 round 6mm white pearls
19 round 6mm gold beads
1⅓ yards of monofilament nylon
1 gold 7mm jump ring
1 gold 7mm spring ring
2 gold calotte crimps

earrings:
4 round 4mm gold beads
24 round 6mm white pearls
14 round 6mm gold beads
1⅓ yards of monofilament nylon
2 gold calotte crimps
2 gold fish hook ear wires

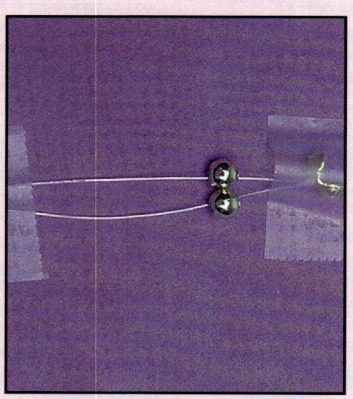

1

1 Choker: Cut the nylon into two 4-foot lengths and knot together 1" from one end. Seal the knot with clear nail polish, let dry and trim off the 1" ends. Slip the long ends through the hole of a calotte, pulling the knot to the inside. Tape the crimp to the work surface and thread a 4mm bead onto each strand.

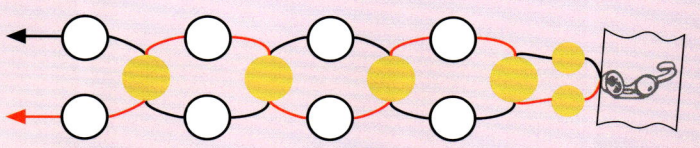

2

2 Follow the diagram to string the 6mm beads. The beading will end with a gold bead; there will be one 6mm white bead remaining for step 4.

3

4

3 Thread a 4mm bead onto each strand, then pass both strands through the remaining calotte. Knot, seal and trim as in step 1. Close both calottes.

4 Join the ten jump rings in a chain (see inside the front cover). Hook one calotte hook through one end of the chain and close the hook. Thread the last 6mm bead onto the head pin, trim the pin ¼" above the bead and use round-nose pliers to form the cut end into a loop. Attach it to the other end of the jump ring chain. Attach the clasp hook to the other calotte and hook at the desired point in the chain.

5

5 Bracelet: Follow steps 1–3 for the choker, but cut the nylon into two 2-foot lengths. String all the beads. Hook one calotte through the eye of the spring ring and the other through the jump ring. Hook the spring ring through the jump ring to clasp the bracelet.

6 Cut the nylon into two 24" lengths. **For each earring:** String a 6mm bead to the center of a nylon length. Follow the diagram to string beads each way from the center.

6

7

7 Thread a 4mm bead onto each strand, then pass both strands through a calotte. Knot, seal and trim as in step 1. Hook the calotte through the eye of an earwire and close.

3

4

Double-Weave Choker & Bracelet

basic supplies
(see inside the front cover)

14" choker:
46 round 4mm gold beads
179 round 6mm white pearls
4 yards of monofilament nylon
2 gold calotte crimps
ten 5mm gold jump rings
1 gold head pin
1 gold hook clasp

7" bracelet:
28 round 4mm gold beads
106 round 4mm white pearls
2 yards of monofilament nylon
2 gold calotte crimps
one 7mm gold jump rings
one 7mm gold spring ring

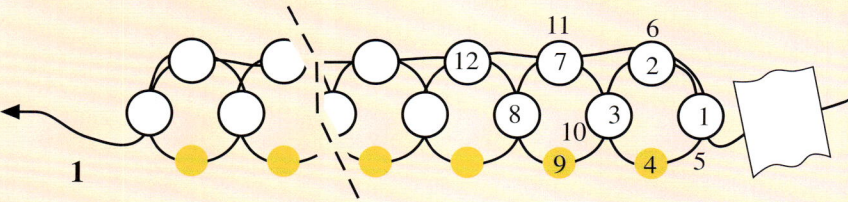

1 **Choker:** Cut the nylon into two 6-foot lengths. Lay one on a flat surface and tape it down 4" from the right end. Follow the diagram to string beads until you have used 44 gold and 89 white beads. End by passing the nylon end again through the last pearl and taping it down.

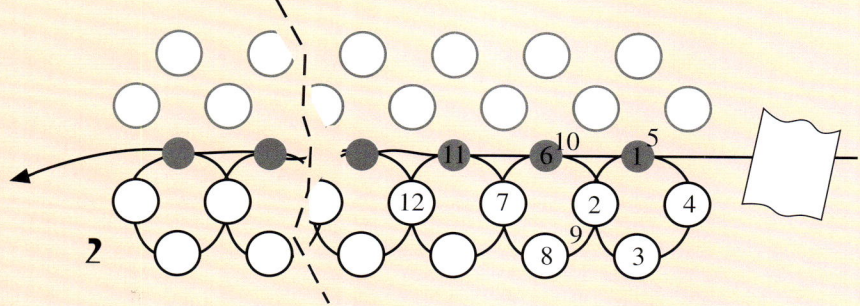

2 Tape the second nylon length below the first and follow the diagram to bead it, weaving the nylon back through the previous gold beads as shown (the beads worked in step 1 are shown in gray). You will have two gold and one white bead left for finishing.

5

3

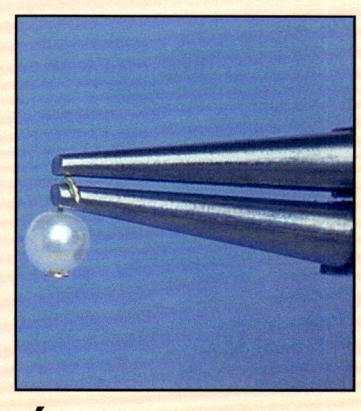
4

3 Untape the finishing end of the first nylon length and hold together with the finishing end of the second length. Pass both through a 4mm gold bead, then through the hole of a calotte. Knot close to the calotte. Seal the knot with nail polish, let dry and trim excess nylon. Untape the beginning ends and finish them in the same way.

4 Join the ten jump rings in a chain (see inside the front cover). Thread the last white bead onto the head pin, trim the pin ¼" above the bead and use round-nose pliers to form the cut end into a loop. Hook the loop through one end of the jump ring chain.

5

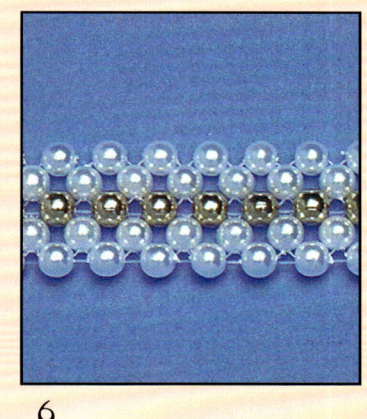
6

5 On one end of the choker, hook the calotte through the free end of the chain and close the hook. Attach the clasp hook to the calotte at the other end of the choker. Hook through the jump rings at the desired length.

6 Bracelet: Follow steps 1–3 for the choker, but cut the nylon into two 3-foot lengths and use only 26 gold beads for the center row.

7 Hook the calotte at one end of the bracelet to the jump ring. Hook the other calotte through the eye of the spring ring.

7

Amber/Teal Choker & Bracelet

The necklace and bracelet shown below are also strung following the basic double-weave pattern shown on pages 4–5. This 14" necklace requires 128 gold 6mm faceted beads, 41 blue 5mm round beads and 41 amber 5mm round

Rounded Spiral Necklace & Bracelet

basic supplies (see inside the front cover)

18" necklace:
57 round 5mm gold beads
57 round 5mm lavender pearls
57 round 5mm white pearls
22 round 8mm white pearls
10 round 6mm gold beads
5 yards of monofilament nylon
2 gold calotte crimps
1 fishhook clasp

7" bracelet:
122 round 4mm white pearls
61 round 4mm pink pearls
4 yards of monofilament nylon
2 gold calotte crimps
one 7mm gold jump ring
one 7mm gold spring ring

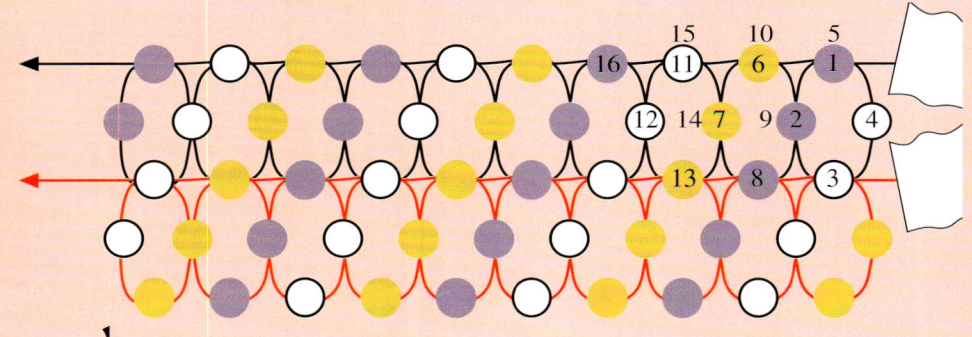

1 **Necklace:** Cut the nylon into three 5-foot lengths. Tape two lengths to the work surface, leaving 10" of each free at the right. Follow the diagram to string 5mm beads in the double-weave pattern (also shown on page 4). Continue until the first, third and fifth rows have 28 beads each and the second and fourth rows contain 29 each.

2 Untape the ends and turn the necklace upside down as shown. The beads will now angle in the opposite direction. Leave the necklace upside down and proceed to step 3.

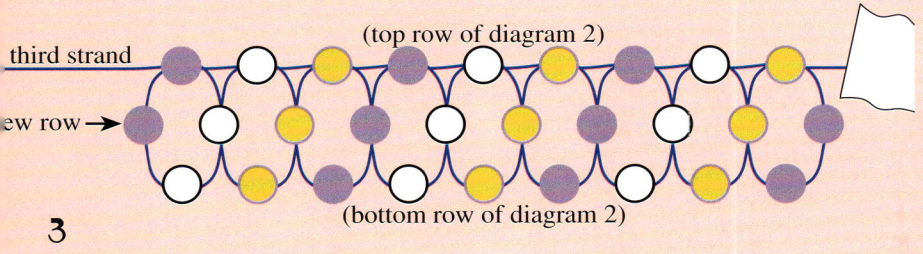

3 Tape the last nylon length on the work surface, leaving 10" extending at the right. Thread the end through the top right gold bead; add another gold bead. Thread it through the bottom right lavender bead, then pick up another lavender bead. Thread it back through the top right gold bead and continue, following the diagram. You are creating one new row which joins the top and bottom rows from the previous step.

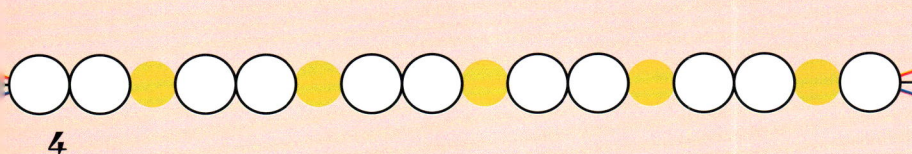

4 On one end of the necklace, hold all three nylon lengths together. Follow the diagram to string 8mm pearls and 6mm gold beads. Pass the nylon ends through the hole of a calotte. Knot close to the calotte, seal the knot with nail polish and let dry. Trim the ends close to the knot and close the calotte. Repeat for the other end of the necklace. Attach one clasp section to each calotte.

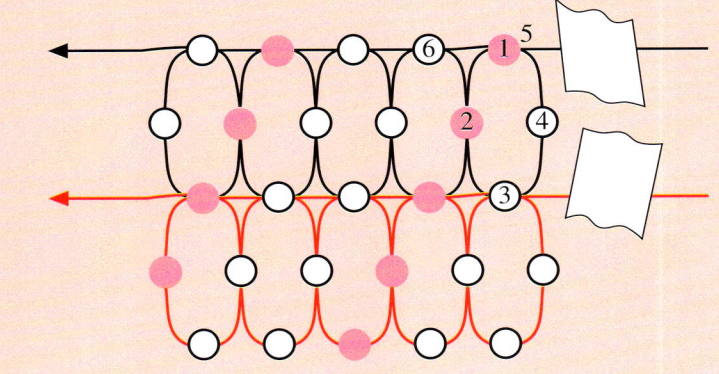

5 Bracelet: Cut the nylon into three 4-foot lengths. Tape two lengths to the work surface, leaving 4" of each free at the right. Follow the diagram to string 4mm beads in the double-weave pattern. Continue until the first, third and fifth rows have 30 beads each and the second and fourth rows contain 31 each.

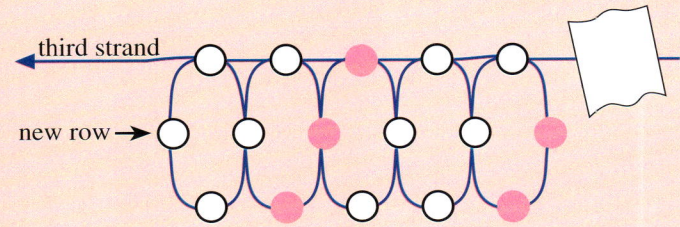

6 Turn the bracelet upside down. Tape the last nylon length on the work surface, leaving 4" extending at the right. Follow the diagram to bead the last connecting row (see step 3). On one end of the bracelet, hold all three nylon lengths together and thread them through the hole of a calotte. Knot close to the calotte, seal the knot with nail polish and let dry. Trim the ends close to the knot and close the calotte. Repeat for the other end of the necklace. Attach the jump ring to one calotte and the spring ring to the other.

8

Extended Double-Weave Necklace & Earrings

basic supplies (see inside the front cover)

18" necklace:
176 round 4mm white pearls
27 round 6mm white pearls
six 7x12mm white pearl teardrops, each with a crosswise hole at the top
131 round 4mm black iridescent beads
11 round 6mm black iridescent beads
6 yards of monofilament nylon
2 gold calotte crimps
1 gold fishhook clasp

earrings:
10 round 4mm white pearls
2 round 6mm white pearls
two 7x12mm white pearl teardrops, each with a crosswise hole at the top
6 round 4mm black iridescent beads
2 round 6mm black iridescent beads
⅔ yard of monofilament nylon
2 gold calotte crimps
2 gold fishhook earwires

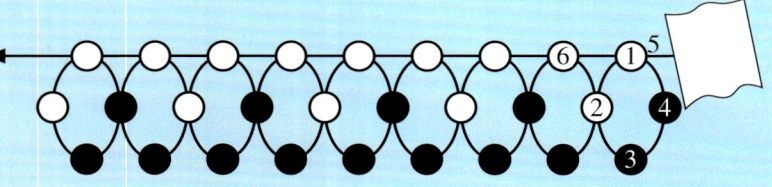

1 **Necklace:** Cut two 8-foot nylon lengths. Tape one to the work surface, leaving 6" free at the right end. Follow the diagram to string 4mm beads and pearls, continuing until the top row has 64 beads.

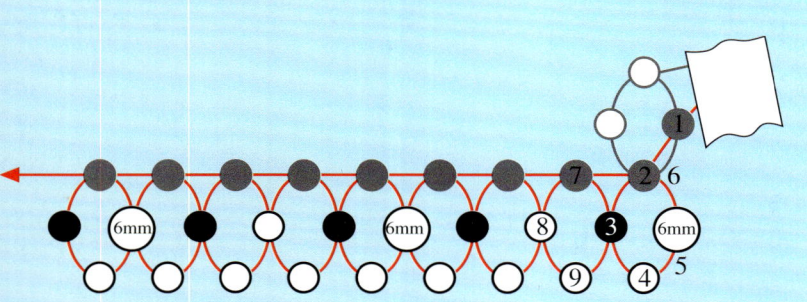

2 Tape the second 8-foot length below the first, leaving 6" free. Thread the end through the first black pearl of the second row. Follow the diagram to bead (beads strung in the previous step are shown in gray).

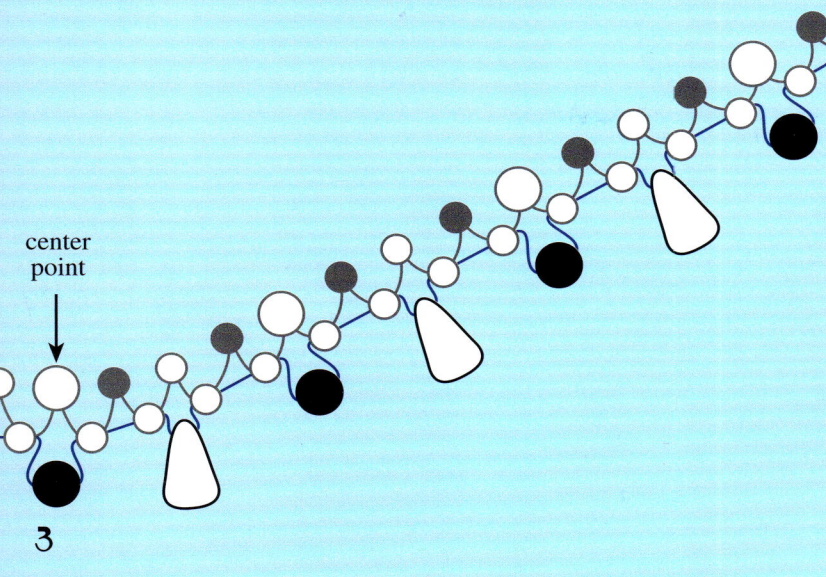

fifth 6mm white pearl →

center point →

3 Tape the remaining 2-foot nylon length below the second length, leaving 6" free. Thread the end through the first black pearl of the second row, the 6mm pearl at the end of the bottom row, and all the pearls along the lower edge until you come to the fifth 6mm pearl. From that point, follow the diagram to the center point of the necklace, then bead in reverse to the opposite end (beads strung in the previous step are shown in gray).

4 Hold all three nylon lengths together at one end and thread them through a 4mm black bead, five 6mm white pearls and the hole of a calotte. Knot close to the calotte. Seal the knot with nail polish, let dry and trim close to the knot; close the calotte. Repeat for the other end. Hook each calotte through one clasp section and close the hooks.

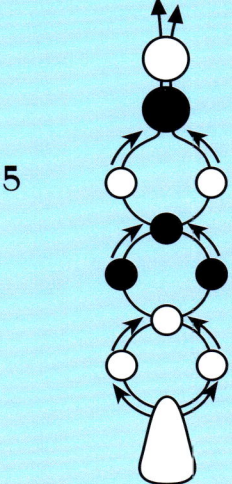

5 Cut the nylon into two 12" lengths. **For each earring:** Slide a teardrop to the center of a nylon length. Follow the diagram to bead both ways from the center. Bring both ends of the nylon through a calotte; knot, seal and trim. Close the calotte and hook through the eye of an earwire.

Flat Hoop Earrings

20 round 6mm white pearls
20 round 6mm gold beads
24 round 4mm black iridescent beads
1 1/3 yards of monofilament nylon
2 calotte crimps
2 fishhook earwires
basic supplies (see inside the front cover)

1 Cut the nylon into two 24" lengths. **For each earring:** String a 4mm bead onto the center of a nylon length, then bead both ways from the center as shown in the diagram. Bring both nylon ends back to the beginning and string them from opposite directions through the first 4mm bead.

2 Pull the nylon ends tight, drawing the beaded band up into a loop. String a 4mm bead onto each strand, then pass both through the hole of a calotte; knot. Seal the knot with nail polish, let dry and trim close to the knot. Close the calotte and hook onto an earwire.

Fan Earrings

14 round 5mm white pearls
10 round 6mm black iridescent beads
38 round 4mm gold beads
1 1/3 yards of monofilament nylon
2 gold calotte crimps
2 fishhook earwires
basic supplies (see inside the front cover)

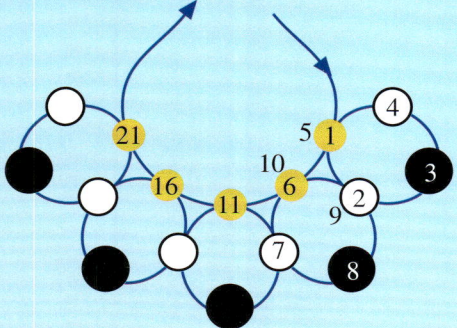

1 Cut the nylon into two 24" lengths. **For each earring:** Tape one to the work surface, leaving 6" free at the right. Follow the diagram to string the beads.

2 String four 4mm beads onto each end of the strand. Hold the nylon ends together and string three 4mm beads, a 5mm pearl and another 4mm bead over both strands. Pass both strands through the hole of a calotte. Knot close to the calotte. Seal the knot with nail polish, let dry and trim the ends close to the knot. Close the calotte and hook onto an earwire.

Pearls with a Center Stone

11

basic supplies (see inside the front cover)

16" necklace:
8 round 4mm white pearls
128 round 6mm white pearls
1 round 10mm clear blue bead
4 round 4mm gold beads
2⅔ yards of monofilament nylon
2 gold calotte crimps
1 gold barrel clasp

7" bracelet:
16 round 4mm white pearls
50 round 6mm white pearls
5 round 10mm clear blue beads
20 round 4mm gold beads
1⅓ yards of monofilament nylon
2 gold calotte crimps
one 7mm gold jump ring
one 7mm gold spring ring

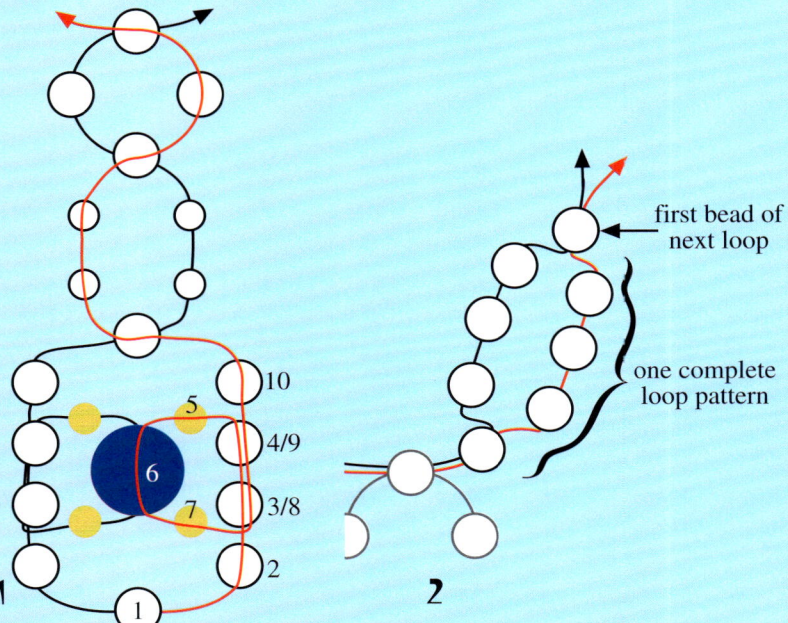

1 Necklace: Cut the nylon into two 4-foot lengths. Slide one 6mm white pearl to the center of one length. Follow the diagram to bead the pendant. (Note: Although one continuous strand is used, for clarity the right half is shown in red as if it lay on top of the beads. Follow the right side number sequence on the left also.)

2 Insert the second nylon length (shown in red) through the top pendant pearl and center it—there should now be two nylon ends extending from each side of this bead. Follow the diagram to string the loop pattern eight times on each side.

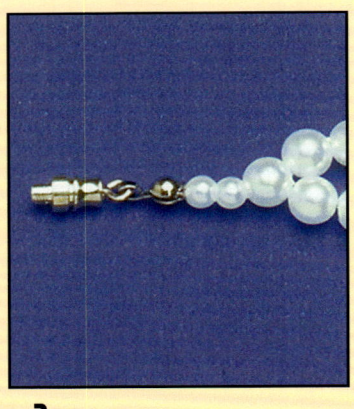

3

3 On one end of the necklace, bring the nylon strands together and string one 6mm and two 4mm pearls. Bring both strands through the hole of a calotte. Knot close to the calotte, seal the knot with nail polish and let dry. Trim the nylon ends close to the knot. Close the calotte and hook through one clasp section. Repeat on the other end of the necklace.

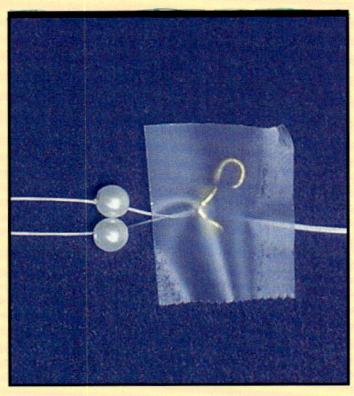

4

4 Bracelet: Cut the nylon into two 24" lengths. Hold the lengths together and knot 1" from one end. Seal the knot with nail polish; let dry. Pass the long ends through the hole of a calotte and pull the knot up snugly inside the calotte. Tape the 1" ends and calotte to the work surface. Separate the strands and string two 4mm pearls up to the calotte on each strand.

5 Follow the diagram to bead one loop pattern (the beads strung in step 4 are shown in gray). Repeat for a total of five loops.

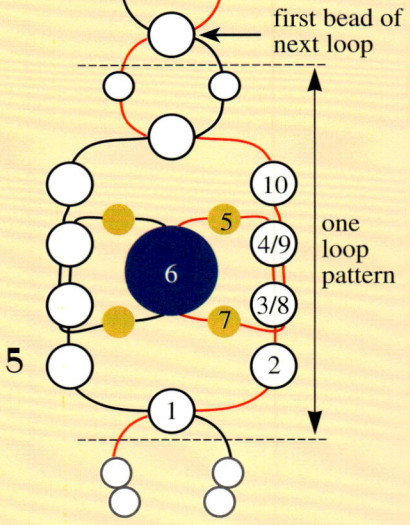

5

6

6 Add one more 4mm pearl to each strand so the bracelet end matches the beginning. Pass both strands through the hole of a calotte. Knot close to the calotte, seal the knot with nail polish and let dry. Untape the bracelet and trim all the nylon ends close to the knots. Close the calottes. Hook one calotte through the jump ring and the other through the eye of the spring ring.

Green & Gold Necklace & Bracelet

basic supplies (see inside the front cover)

16" necklace:
98 round 8mm antique gold beads
one 12mm black/gold patterned lantern bead
24 round faceted 4mm gold beads
2⅔ yards of monofilament nylon
2 gold calotte crimps
1 gold barrel clasp

7" bracelet:
27 round 8mm antique gold beads
four 12mm black/gold patterned lantern beads
24 round faceted 4mm gold beads
1⅓ yards of monofilament nylon
2 gold calotte crimps
one 7mm gold jump ring
one 7mm gold spring ring

Follow the directions for the necklace and bracelet on pages 11–12, noting these changes:

Necklace:
(A) Omit the two 4mm pearls between the last loop pattern and the calotte on each end (page 12, step 3).

(B) Substitute 8mm antique gold beads for 6mm white pearls.

(C) String the loop pattern only seven times on each side of the necklace.

(D) Use a faceted gold bead when bringing the two strands together between loops.

(E) Substitute a faceted gold bead for each 4mm gold bead and each 4mm pearl.

(F) Substitute a lantern bead for the blue bead.

Bracelet:
(G) Substitute a faceted bead for each 4mm gold bead and each 4mm pearl.

(H) Substitute 8mm antique gold beads for 6mm white pearls.

(I) Substitute lantern beads for blue beads.

(J) Omit the two 4mm pearls and the extra 6mm pearl between loop patterns.

(K) Repeat the loop pattern only four times.

14 Tube Necklace, Bracelet & Earrings

basic supplies (see inside the front cover)

24" necklace:
303 round 4mm white pearls
100 round 4mm black iridescent beads
100 round 4mm gold beads
100 round 4mm silver beads
10 yards of monofilament nylon
2 gold calotte crimps
1 gold 7mm jump ring
1 gold clasp hook

7" bracelet:
87 round 4mm white pearls
28 round 4mm black iridescent beads
28 round 4mm gold beads
28 round 4mm silver beads
4 yards of monofilament nylon
2 gold calotte crimps
1 gold 7mm jump ring
1 gold 7mm spring ring

2½" long earrings:
60 round 4mm white pearls
18 round 4mm black iridescent beads
18 round 4mm gold beads
18 round 4mm silver beads
2 round 6mm white pearls
4 yards of monofilament nylon
2 gold calotte crimps
2 gold fishhook earwires

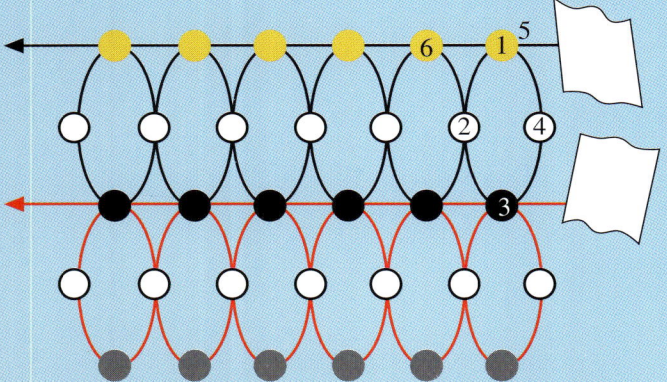

1 Necklace: Cut the nylon into three 10-foot lengths. Tape two lengths to the work surface, leaving 4" of each free at the right. Follow the diagram to string beads in the double-weave pattern (also shown on page 4), continuing until there are 100 beads in the first, third and fifth rows and 101 beads in the second and fourth rows.

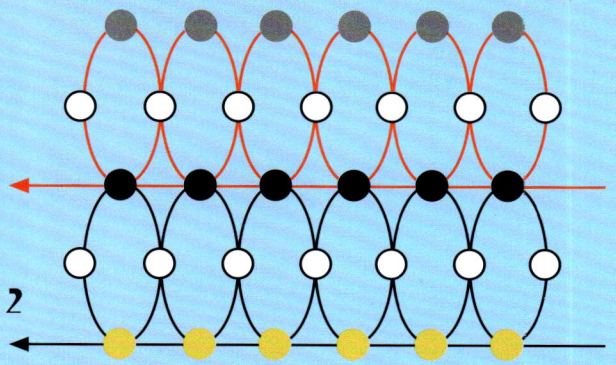

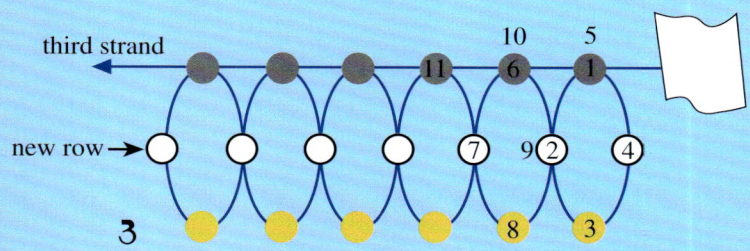

2 Untape the ends and turn the necklace upside down as shown.

3 Tape down the last nylon length, leaving 6" free at the right. Pass the leading end through the first silver bead and string on a white pearl. Pass it through the first gold bead and string another pearl, then bring it back through the first silver bead. Continue, following the diagram, until all the beads are used. Pass the nylon ends through the hole of a calotte. Knot close to the calotte, seal the knot with nail polish and let dry. Trim the ends close to the calotte and close the calotte. Untape the other end of the necklace and repeat. Attach the clasp hook to one calotte hook and the jump ring to the other.

4 **Bracelet:** Cut the nylon into three 48" lengths. Follow steps 1–3, but use 28 beads in the first, third and fifth rows and 29 beads in the second and fourth rows. Use the spring ring in place of the clasp hook.

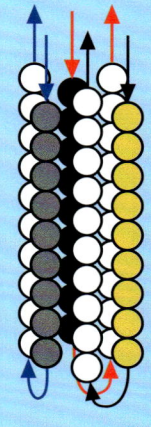

5 **Earrings:** Cut the nylon into six 24" lengths. For each earring, follow steps 1–3, but use 9 beads in the first, third and fifth rows and 10 beads in the second, fourth and joining rows. Thread each nylon length back through an entire row of pearls, ending with all six nylon ends at the top.

6 Pass all six nylon ends through a 6mm pearl, then through the hole of a calotte. Knot close to the calotte, seal the knot with nail polish and let dry. Trim the ends close to the calotte and close the calotte. Hook it onto the eye of an earwire.

Chinese Coin Knot Pendant

100 round 4mm white pearls
100 round 4mm gold beads
one 8mm round white pearl
1⅓ yards of 34-gauge gold beading wire
1 gold calotte crimp
one 20" gold chain with clasp
ball-headed straight pins
dab of modeling clay
basic supplies (see inside the front cover)

DESIGNER'S NOTE: The double coin knot is a decorative knot usually made with cords, a symbol of prosperity. The shape derives from an ancient Chinese coin, hence the name. You may wish to practice the knot with cord before making this beaded wire version.

1 Cut the wire into two 24" lengths; twist together 3" from one end. String all the 4mm pearls onto one wire and all the gold beads onto the other. Push the beads close together and wrap a bit of modeling clay around each wire below the last bead to prevent them from sliding down. Measure along the beads 2" from the twist in the wires and tape this point to your work surface with the twist nearest to you and the clay ends extending away from you. The knot will be worked upside down.

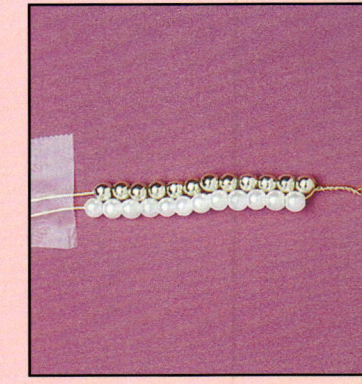

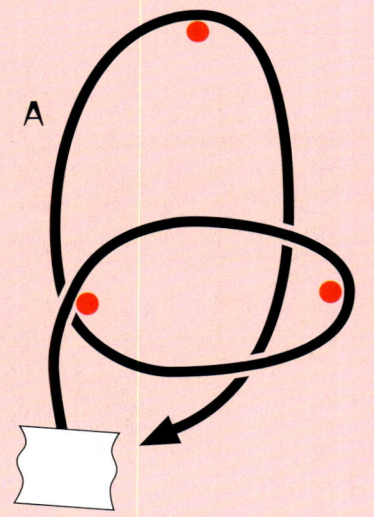
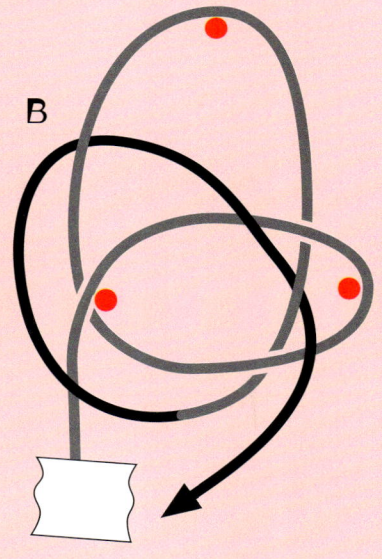

2 Holding both strands together, follow diagrams A and B to work the knot, securing each turn with a pin as illustrated by the red dots.

3 Even the knot by tightening the loops in the order they were made. Unpin the knot, untape the wire ends and discard the clay. Untwist the beginning wire ends and hold all four ends together. Remove beads from one end if necessary to make the knot symmetrical. Twist all four wire ends together. Pass them through the 8mm pearl, then through the hole in the calotte. Knot the wires close to the calotte and seal the knot with nail polish. Let dry; trim excess wire and close the calotte. Hook it to the center of the chain.